⋆DR MAYA⋆

ICE CREAM
SCIENTIST

The Look Up Series #3

DR MAYA

ICE CREAM SCIENTIST

Real Women in S.T.E.A.M.

Aubre Andrus

ADJECTIVE
ANIMAL
PUBLISHING

LOOK
UP
SERIES

"FOR THE GIRLS WHO ALWAYS DREAM ABOUT WHAT THEY'LL BE ONE DAY." — AA

Published by Adjective Animal Publishing in Santa Monica, California.

Visit us online at adjectiveanimalpublishing.com.

Design: Alice Connew
Photography: Ariel Moore
Logos: Shay Merritté
Illustrations: Aubre Andrus

6, Paper clip illustration: Designed by rawpixel.com/Freepik; 6, Polaroid: Roland Deason/Unsplash; 9, Candy bins: Matt Schwartz/Unsplash; 11 Rolled ice cream, Etienne Voss/iStock; 12, St Louis: Brittany Butler/Unsplash; 12, Los Angeles: Pedro Marroquin/Unsplash; 13, Dog eating ice cream: Christian Bowen/Unsplash; 14, Maya in Lab: Jeff Miller/University of Wisconsin-Madison; 14, Chocolate chip ice cream: American Heritage Chocolate/Unsplash; 16, Strawberries and ice cream: Kenta Kikuchi/Unsplash; 17, Ice cream machine, Cesare Ferrari/iStock; 22, Baby holding ice cream: Patrick Fore/Unsplash; 26, Carleton College: Dogs1337, Wikimedia; 26, Science Hall, University of Wisconsin-Madison: File Upload Bot (Dori) , Wikimedia; 32, Three hands holding ice cream: Mark Cruz/Unsplash; 32, Leaning tower of Pisa: Jakob Owens/Unsplash; 41, Neon ice cream: Leonardo Sanches/Unsplash; 41, Ice cream solves everything: Brendan Church/Unsplash; 41, Polaroid: Rochelle Lee/Unsplash; 44, Ice cream prop: Ekaterina Tyapkina/Unsplash; 54, Paper clip illustration: Designed by rawpixel.com/Freepik; 54, Polaroid: Roland Deason/Unsplash

Library of Congress Cataloging-in-Publication Data is available upon request.

ISBN 9781639460106 (paperback)
ISBN 9781639460113 (hardcover)
ISBN 9781639460120 (e-book)

TABLE OF CONTENTS

CHAPTER 1
MEET DR. MAYA

✒ICE CREAM DREAMS ✒

What makes you happy? For me, it's ice cream!

I'm Doctor Maya, and I'm an ice cream scientist. I had never met an ice cream scientist before I became one. Now I know everything about the science behind frozen desserts. YUM!

Everyone eats food. But as a food scientist, I study the **science of food**. That includes what food is made of, how to make foods that are safe and nutritious, how to package food so it stays fresh, and how to make cool new food products and flavors.

Because I specialize in ice cream, I can tell you how ice crystals are formed, how different kinds of sugars can change the texture of ice cream, and why ice cream melts. It's sweet science!

There are many different kinds of food scientists like cheese scientists, candy scientists, and meat scientists. Food scientists can use their knowledge to start their own food company, create machines that make food products, develop a specific kind of food, and more.

You can thank food scientists for delicious treats like toaster pastries. Someone had to figure out how to fill a rectangular pastry with jelly and top it off with frosting and sprinkles. Then package it so it could be eaten weeks later—and still taste good!

Food scientists are always trying to **SOLVE PROBLEMS**. How can we make food last longer? How can we make it taste better? And, most importantly, how can we make food more nutritious? Food scientists create the nutrition labels that you see on the side of packages. **They make sure the food we eat keeps us healthy and strong**.

Today, food scientists are inventing so many creative products like milk made from oats, burgers made from plants, and pizza dough made from cauliflower. Not only do these products taste good, but they can be more nutritious and better for the environment. Scientists have even created no-waste packaging from mushrooms that can decompose, or break down, completely.

DOCTOR VS DOCTOR

I have a PhD (pronounce each letter: "P" "H" "D"), which is a degree that I earned after doing years of scientific research. It's different from a doctor of medicine, which is a degree students earn after going to medical school. After earning either degree, you earn the title of "Doctor."

✦ EXPRESS YOURSELF ✦

Although ice cream is a science, it's **TRULY AN ART** as well. That's what makes it so magical. I consider myself an artist because ice cream is a blank canvas. I can add colors, flavors, and textures. I'm just an artist in a science lab instead of an art studio.

Even though I'm not great at drawing, painting, or music, I love to create. Science requires a lot of CREATIVITY! Right now, I'm having fun creating flavors for a new ice cream company. I love to walk the aisles of a grocery store and look at the flavors of drinks, candy, and yogurt for inspiration.

One day, I walked through a garden and the pink roses inspired me to make a pink tea flavor. Another time I was inspired by a popular American dish called cornbread. I mixed cornbread, blackberry jam, honey, and salt into ice cream. It was amazing! Most people were unsure of this flavor but they loved it after the first bite.

As a scientist, I'm always thinking about something in a new way. I'm always asking myself, *How can I take something simple and make it different?* That's how my cookies and cream flavor became such a hit. We made one thing different—**IT'S PURPLE**! People "eat" with their eyes first. And purple ice cream certainly catches their eyes.

I can make ice cream taste like anything. I've taken wacky things that people didn't even know they wanted and put it into ice cream. Think ketchup ice cream, garlic ice cream, tomato basil ice cream, cheese ice cream, and more!

FLAVOR SCIENCE

The most popular flavors in the U.S. are vanilla, chocolate, and strawberry closely followed by butter pecan, mint chocolate chip, and cookies and cream. In other countries like Italy and Turkey, pistachio is a very popular flavor. In Asian countries, frozen desserts are sometimes flavored with rose water or a spice called saffron.

Ice cream isn't just a single scoop on a cone—think about ice cream bars, ice cream floats, banana splits, ice cream sandwiches, and ice cream sundaes! There is so much you can do with ice cream. In Thailand, **rolled ice cream** became really popular in 2009. Now people all over the world are eating it.

Rolled ice cream is made-to-order on a very cold, rectangular pan. A liquid ice cream mix is poured over toppings then smoothed flat with a spatula as it **FREEZES FAST**. Next, it's cut into thin slices that are rolled into tubes then placed in a cup. Who knew that there were still amazing new creations that you can make with ice cream?!

Ice cream scientists get to have fun, be creative, and be inspired by the world around them. And, of course, make people smile. Because who doesn't love ice cream?

ALL ABOUT
DR. MAYA

I'm from...
St. Louis, MO

But now I live in...
Los Angeles, CA

MAYA'S FAVORITES

Food:
Ice cream - of course!

Place:
The world! I can't pick!

Ice Cream Flavor:
Anything with
OREO® cookies!

Color:
White

Birthday:
February 10

Siblings:
I have an older
brother and sister

Chocolate or vanilla?
Vanilla

Singing or dancing?
Dancing

Summer or winter?
Winter

Ocean or mountains?
Ocean

TV or movies?
TV

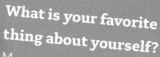

What is your favorite thing about yourself?
My energy—it's contagious! I have an ability to inspire others with both my creativity and my passion.

Dog or cat?
Dogs

Morning or evening?
Morning

TV or movies?
Movies

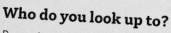

Who do you look up to?
People who are creative, aren't afraid to take risks, and want to make the world a better place.

Dr. Maya Warren
Ice Cream Expert

CHAPTER 2
HOW ICE CREAM GETS MADE

CHURN, BABY CHURN

Ice cream is one of the most complicated sciences known to humans—it's a solid, liquid, and gas all in one! There are ice crystals (which are solids), air bubbles (which are gas), and a little bit of liquid that we can't see.

To make ice cream, I start with a **LIQUID ICE CREAM MIX**. It's basically a sweetened cream with just the right amount of sugar, solids, and fat droplets. It sounds like a recipe, but it's actually a balanced chemical equation. It won't freeze unless you have just the right amount of ingredients.

IT ALL ADDS UP

To make ice cream, it's all about balancing a chemical equation. Chemical equations are numbers and symbols that are written down to show how things react when they are mixed together. It's kind of like a math problem. For example, I can use an equation to help me figure out how much sugar I should add based on the amount of ice cream I'm making. If I add too much sugar, the ice cream might end up soupy when exiting the freezer and loose and sticky when scooping. If too little sugar is added, it might be too hard. So balancing the "ice cream equation" is key to making a delicious and creamy product.

Once I've perfected my liquid ice cream mix, I don't freeze it yet. **I HEAT IT UP!** The heat helps kill any germs. Next, I squeeze it through a small funnel. The pressure breaks up the fat droplets and makes the liquid really smooth. Finally, I let the liquid mix cool in the refrigerator. Now I have a blank canvas to play with! This is called the **ice cream base**.

The ice cream base is now ready for the best part—flavor! I can add anything from cookie crumbles to vanilla flavoring. How much flavor I add will affect the taste. But flavor can affect the texture, too. For example, a strawberry paste has lots of sugar. This added sugar will alter the chemical equation of my ice cream base. It will make the ice cream softer.

Now it's time for the really cool science to begin. I put the ice cream base into an ice cream machine, which is a cold barrel with a rotating blade inside. The water in the mix starts to freeze and stick to the sides of the barrel. Then, the blade scoops the ice crystals off the side of the barrel. Now the ice cream is forming! This process is called churning.

At the same time, the blade helps whip air into the ice cream. Air is a very important ingredient in ice cream. Slowly but surely, all of the liquid will turn into ice cream. It's a unique mix of fat, water, sugar, ice, and air bubbles—and it tastes delicious.

AIRTIME

You can put a melted tub of ice cream back in the freezer, but it will never have the same texture again. That's because a key ingredient—air bubbles—have collapsed. Ice cream with lots of air bubbles tends to melt faster.

TESTING, 1, 2, 3!

Now that my ice cream is complete, I'll do a taste test. Flavors develop over time, so I'll check my ice cream over the next few days to see if anything has changed. If my ice cream had inclusions, which are pieces of food like cookie crumbles, I'll want to check on those too.

After one day, a cookie crumble might be nice and crunchy. But three days later, it might soften. It can get soggy if it starts soaking up the water in the ice cream. **This is called moisture migration.** Not all moisture migration is bad though. For example, a soggy but frozen chocolate sandwich cookie is delicious! That's why I love ice cream with crushed up chocolate sandwich cookies so much.

I don't make the flavors or inclusions. I buy them. This is called 'sourcing.' I'm always on the look-out for cool ingredients that I can mix into ice cream. I also consider how much they cost. I don't want expensive ingredients because then we'd have to charge the customer more.

POPULAR INCLUSIONS

Small pieces of brownie or cake

Jams and Jellies

Cookie crumbles

Sprinkles

Fruit pieces

Sweet sauces like Chocolate, Caramel, or Honey

Crushed nuts

If I don't like how the ice cream turned out, I'll start over. I might choose a different ingredient or mix in more or less flavor. I always ask friends, family, and coworkers to try a new flavor I'm working on. Their feedback is important to me. After all, I want to make ice cream that everyone loves.

After lots of taste testing, I'll settle on a perfect flavor. Then I can start thinking about the selling process. What will I name this ice cream? What will the packaging look like? What should the photo shoot look like? Not all food scientists get to take part in this, but I work for a small ice cream company, so I do.

It's so cool to see my ice cream sitting on shelf at a grocery store or watching people take a bite of one of my creations at a scoop shop. So many people have good memories of eating ice cream. I love that I can play a small part in making those memories.

What is your favorite memory that involves ice cream?

FROM IDEA TO ICE CREAM

2. The liquid ice cream mix gets heated up to kill bacteria.

1. Ice cream starts with a liquid mix. It's a balance of sugar, solids, and fat droplets.

3. The liquid mix is squeezed through a funnel. The pressure helps break up the fat droplets to make a smooth mix.

4. The mix is cooled for four to twenty four hours where it "ages." This means that all the ingredients have time to settle together and start working their magic.

5. The ice cream mix is flavored. Inclusions, like cookie crumbles or caramel ribbons, can be added here.

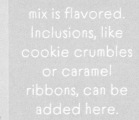

8. The ice cream is almost done. The blade continues to rotate, whipping air bubbles into the mix.

9. Time for a taste test. Does the ice cream meet our expectations? If not, we can start over.

7. The liquid starts freezing to the sides of the barrel. The blade scrapes the frozen liquid off the sides of the wall. This is ice cream!

10. Yum! Our ice cream is complete. Cup or a cone?

6. The mix is poured into an ice cream machine with a frozen barrel and a rotating blade. This process is called churning.

I ♡ CHEMISTRY

CHAPTER 3
HOW DID I GET HERE?

brownies

$4 \times 3 = 12$
$6 \times 6 = 36$
$8 \times 9 = 72$

✐ SCHOOL DAYS ✐

When I was younger, you could find me bouncing around and playing outside all day in St. Louis, Missouri. I liked to dig in the dirt and pretend that I was fossil hunting. I couldn't sit still. I had a lot of ENERGY!

To me, there was nothing better than learning and exploring. Even as a little kid, **I ALWAYS WANTED TO SHINE**. I wanted to be great at something. I didn't know exactly what that something would be. It was just a feeling that I had.

When I was six years old, I loved using my little plastic microwave toy that really worked. I peered into the window and watched the mix that I just stirred bake into brownies. I was so intrigued.

I even remember making ice cream for the very first time. I had an ice cream maker that was designed especially for little kids. The ice cream tasted terrible! I had accidentally let the salty water mix get into the ice cream. **Oops!** But I had so much fun making it.

I also loved to play with slime and do experiments. My parents eventually signed me up for a robotics camp. I couldn't believe that **I COULD BUILD MY OWN ROBOT**. When I clapped, it turned on and moved. When I clapped again, it turned off. So cool!

In school, I did really well in science and math. I thought timed multiplication tests were **thrilling**. In eighth grade, I began tutoring younger kids. I liked using my skills to give back. It was important to me that I shared my talent with others and not keep it all inside.

Writing and spelling were always more challenging for me. But I knew I had to work hard at these subjects because they were connected to science. In science classes, you need to be able to write a good hypothesis. I realized that just because I was good at science, it didn't mean that I was good at all parts of science. There was always room for me to improve.

FUN FACT!

A hypothesis is an educated guess based on what you know. You can do an experiment to test your hypothesis, gather results, and see if you were correct.

In school, I played basketball, did gymnastics, and was class president. It wasn't until high school that I really fell in love with science—**chemistry to be exact.** In chemistry, you get to study what things are made of and why. I learned about what makes up our bodies and the world around us. It was amazing!

I had a great chemistry teacher. He allowed me to see the BEAUTY in loving science. I didn't know any other students who loved science as much as I did. But it didn't matter. I loved what I loved! Even though I was good at science and had a passion for chemistry, I still had to work hard and motivate myself to finish all my homework. If you want to be great at something, it takes a lot of effort.

Until then, I had always thought I'd go to college to become a sports medicine doctor. But now it was clear to me what I should study: chemistry! I couldn't wait to get to college and learn more about science. And who knows? Maybe one day I'd become a chemistry teacher.

DR. MAYA'S UNIVERSITY

School: Carleton College
Location: Northfield, Minnesota
Major: Chemistry

School: University of Wisconsin-Madison
Location: Madison, Wisconsin
Major: PhD, Food Science

FUN FACT!

The University of Wisconsin makes their very own ice cream right on campus. Students especially love to pick up a scoop of Babcock Ice Cream's berry flavor, "Blue Moon".

Carleton College in Minnesota is where I studied Chemistry

This is the University of Wisconsin-Madison's Science Hall

ℓ DOCTOR OF ℓ
ICE CREAM

Four years of studying chemistry at Carleton College flew by! Before I knew it, my time in Minnesota was coming to an end. Just before I graduated, I happened to tune into a TV show that was all about how food gets made. They were making flavored sodas that tasted like Thanksgiving dinner. They called it "**food science**." I had never heard of it before!

I thought about how much I had loved making ice cream and brownies as a kid. Now I knew why I loved it so much—it was food science! I wanted to learn more about it. I applied to a food science program at the University of Wisconsin in Madison and got in!

When I first stepped into the lab, I saw a group of students wearing white lab coats and watching ice cream melt. *We can study ice cream?* I thought. Then I knew it—I wanted to study the science of ice cream. I wanted to make predictions about why ice cream melted a certain way. I wanted to hold taste testing panels and ask people how ice cream felt in their mouths. I wanted to spend years researching ice cream then make batches of my own flavors. **I WANTED TO BECOME DR. MAYA, ICE CREAM SCIENTIST.**

COOL FOOD SCIENCE DISCOVERIES

SEAWEED SIPPERS
At the 2019 London Marathon, runners were handed water-filled pouches made from seaweed instead of plastic bottles. The seaweed pouches are edible or can be thrown away, where they will be naturally broken down in four to six weeks. A great solution to plastic pollution!

DOWNLOAD YOUR DINNER
What do chocolate and pizza have in common? Both can be printed on a 3D printer! Scientists and engineers believe 3D food printers, food cartridges, and downloadable designs could be a great solution for feeding astronauts in space but could also help us here on Earth by reducing food waste and creating extra-healthy meals.

MAGIC NOODLES
Imagine a box of flat noodles. Put them in a pot of boiling water and they turn curly! Cool, right? And better for the environment. That's because spiral noodles take up more space in a package than flat noodles. Scientists simply added teeny-tiny grooves to the noodles. Sometimes the smallest discoveries can make a big difference!

✑ A DEGREE FOR ALL ✑

My mom got her PhD in American Studies when I was in eighth grade. So, education was always very important in my family. But when I told my parents that I was going to get my PhD in ice cream, they said, "Excuse me. You're going to do what?!"

It hadn't always been my dream to get a PhD. But it had been a dream of mine to be great. And now I knew that I was going to **be great at ice cream**. I studied ice cream for seven years. I traveled to Paris to research frozen desserts and worked with many different ice cream companies along the way. Over time, I became an ice cream expert.

I'm so proud of my PhD, especially because I earned it in a subject that **I LOVE SO DEARLY**. It became more than a PhD for me. It's a degree for everyone who was once told they couldn't do something. It's for anyone who aspires to do great things and think outside the box. It's a degree of possibility.

WHAT IS A PHD?

Dr. Maya has a PhD degree. Here's what that means and why she earned it.

After high school, people can choose to go to college to learn more about a specific career. It takes about four years to earn an undergraduate degree. Instead of applying for jobs after college, some people apply to a master's program, which can take a few years to finish, or a doctorate program, which can take five years or more to complete.

Students who complete a doctorate program earn a PhD, which is also known as a Doctor of Philosophy. It's the highest degree you can earn. PhD students do tons of research and teach other students while they complete their degree. Some PhDs go on to become professors at universities.

WHAT IS A JOB?

Dr. Maya's job is 'food scientist.' Why do people like Dr. Maya have a job?

People work at a job in order to make money, which can be used to pay for a place to live, food, clothing, and fun things like travel and entertainment. Jobs give people a sense of purpose, or a reason to use their talents every day. Jobs can also make the world a better place by helping other people or by solving big problems. You can meet cool people and learn new things at a job. Or even travel the world!

Have you ever made money by doing a chore or task?

What are some careers that you can think of?

What kind of jobs do the people in your life have?

A pomegranate at a market in India.

CHAPTER 4
ICE CREAM AROUND THE WORLD

Amazing pyramids in Egypt.

∽ SWEET TRAVELS ∽

I've made ice cream all over the world. When I worked for a big ice cream company, it was my job to open ice cream shops in countries that didn't have an ice cream shop. We couldn't just ship ice cream from the U.S.—it would have **MELTED**! To make traditional ice cream, you need dairy milk. Milk comes from cows. So, if we wanted to open a scoop shop in these countries, we had to help them build a farm first.

That's how I found myself **building dairy farms in Africa**. After we built farms in countries like Kenya and Nigeria, we'd teach people how to use machines to make ice cream. Whenever I open an ice cream shop in a new country, I have to think about what flavors their future customers might like. It's probably different from what I like as an American.

I noticed a lot of people drinking a **PASSIONFRUIT SODA** in Nairobi, Kenya. So, I said, "Why don't we make an ice cream flavor out of this soda?" We did it and everyone loved it. It's cool to know that I helped grow a business in Kenya. I made an impact on them, but they also made an impact on me. I'll never forget the memories, friendships, and experiences I had there.

TYPES OF FROZEN DESSERTS

ICE CREAM

To legally call a product ice cream, it must be made from at least ten percent diary fat. Dairy fat is the fat that comes from milk and cream. Ice cream is churned fast, which gives it a lot of air bubbles and makes it fluffier in texture.

SOFT-SERVE ICE CREAM

Soft-serve is made from the same ingredients as traditional ice cream, but the machine it's dispensed from gives it a smoother texture. The machine adds more air and keeps the ice cream at a warmer temperature.

GELATO

Gelato is Italian for 'ice cream' but it's not quite the same. It has less cream and is churned at a slower speed, which means it has less air. That makes it dense. It's also kept at a warmer temperature, which makes it softer and quicker to melt on your tongue.

FROZEN YOGURT

"Fro yo" is made the same way as ice cream but yogurt is added as a key ingredient.

FROZEN CUSTARD

Custard uses the same ice cream base as ice cream, but egg yolk is added. The egg yolk makes it thicker and softer, almost more like soft-serve ice cream.

SORBET

Sorbet is made from fruit and sugar—there's no milk! Because it's made in an ice cream maker, it's soft and scoopable. But it's not creamy like ice cream.

SHERBET

If you mixed sorbet and ice cream, you'd get sherbet! It's like sorbet, which is made of fruit and sugar, but with a little bit of cream added.

LIQUID NITROGEN ICE CREAM

Liquid nitrogen can freeze an ice cream base in minutes—it's -320 degrees Fahrenheit (-160 degrees Celsius)! When ice cream is frozen so quickly, it allows the ice crystals to remain very small, which results in creamy ice cream.

✒ LET'S EXPLORE ✒

During my work travels, I've visited an elephant orphanage, kissed a giraffe, and went on safari to see lions, zebras, and rhinos. I got to travel to Pakistan as well as Brazil, India, Taiwan, Thailand, Egypt, and more.

My favorite part about traveling is learning. **I love to visit markets** and see the hustle and bustle. It's where all the local people come every day to buy their groceries or make a living by selling food and other products. In Brazil, I saw amazing exotic fruits and wondered, "What is this? This is so interesting!"

I've eaten stinky tofu in Taiwan and stood in a shop in India with hundreds of colorful scarves with beautiful embroidery. I bought my FAVORITE pair of sandals in Pakistan that were made by hand. It's amazing how much you can learn about the local people when you explore a market in a new place. You may be far away from home, but soon you'll begin seeing more similarities than differences.

Whenever I walk down a street in a new country and see a group of kids, I buy them ice cream. It always makes them so happy. At the end of the day, it doesn't matter what country I'm in. **EVERYONE LOVES ICE CREAM**. Ice cream really is a universal language. It knows no boundaries. Ice cream brings people together like no other food can.

That's one of the reasons why I helped start Ice Cream for Change. It's a nonprofit that uses ice cream for the power of good. **We raised $70,000 on National Ice Cream Day** from more than 100 different ice cream companies and ice cream makers across North America.

We donated the money to education and sports programs that help young African American kids. Ice cream breaks barriers and brings people together, so it was the perfect way to raise money for an important cause. I like to focus on the positive things that I can control. What drives me is my passion, my happiness, and my desire to make an impact.

Can you think of a time that you gave back or helped an important cause?

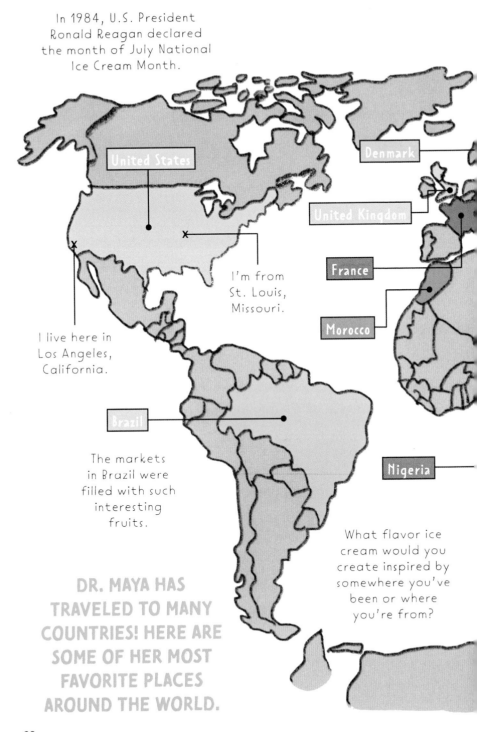

In 1984, U.S. President Ronald Reagan declared the month of July National Ice Cream Month.

United States

Denmark

United Kingdom

France

Morocco

I'm from St. Louis, Missouri.

I live here in Los Angeles, California.

Brazil

The markets in Brazil were filled with such interesting fruits.

Nigeria

What flavor ice cream would you create inspired by somewhere you've been or where you're from?

DR. MAYA HAS TRAVELED TO MANY COUNTRIES! HERE ARE SOME OF HER MOST FAVORITE PLACES AROUND THE WORLD.

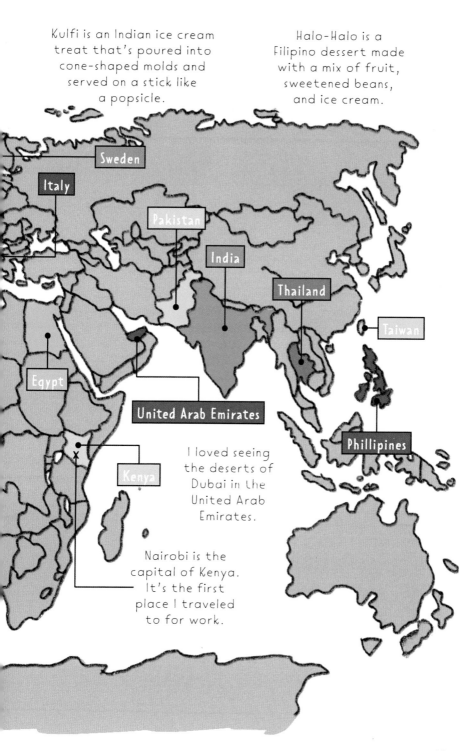

Kulfi is an Indian ice cream treat that's poured into cone-shaped molds and served on a stick like a popsicle.

Halo-Halo is a Filipino dessert made with a mix of fruit, sweetened beans, and ice cream.

Sweden

Italy

Pakistan

India

Thailand

Taiwan

Egypt

United Arab Emirates

Phillipines

I loved seeing the deserts of Dubai in the United Arab Emirates.

Kenya

Nairobi is the capital of Kenya. It's the first place I traveled to for work.

After spending years traveling the globe, I've managed to fall even more in love with ice cream. I love that I've found my passion. Ice cream inspires me every day. I didn't invent

ice cream. I just looked at it through a different lens. It's science! It's possibilities! It's opportunities!

It's also my talent. Just like Serena Willams is an amazing tennis player, I'm an extraordinary ice cream scientist. What is it that you love? Think about what you can do with it that hasn't been done before. Find your path within that passion and own it. But know that it's not just about finding your passion. It's about knowing who you are and what makes you happy.

When I tell people I'm an ice cream scientist, the first thing they do is laugh. I think it's because they can't believe it. It's just a reaction they have to hearing something that is seemingly **UNBELIEVABLE**.

But it doesn't matter who laughs at me because I'm happy. It wasn't necessarily my goal to become an ice cream scientist. **My goal was to be happy!** And I achieve that goal every day. You can run a marathon or code video games or sew your own shirt. You can become an ice cream scientist even though you've never met one before—I did!

When are you most happy?

DR. MAYA'S
ADVICE FOR
YOUNG SCIENTISTS

FOLLOW YOUR PASSION.

No matter what it is—fashion, technology, video games, whatever! When your inner desire and outward passion match up, great things can happen.

lee

BELIEVE IN YOURSELF.

Believe that you can achieve what you want to achieve in life. Believe that you are great and that you have what it takes to make your dreams come true even when things get hard—because they will sometimes!

THINK OUTSIDE THE BOX.

Even if something has never been done before—and even if you've never seen it done by someone who looks like you—find your path and own it.

CHOOSE HAPPINESS.

My goal is to be happy. Being an ice cream scientist makes me happy. I don't care if others laugh when I tell them what I do. It brings me joy and that's all that matters.

DON'T STOP.

I wear a bracelet that says, "She believed she could, so she did." But I like to add to that: "And then she did it again." Achieve in ways you never thought you could achieve, but never stop or settle. Keep going.

CHAPTER 5
YOU CAN BE AN
ICE CREAM SCIENTIST!

ℓ FLAVOR ℓ DEVELOPMENT

Let's dream up your own flavor of ice cream. First, think about all of your favorite flavors, favorite food products, and favorite meals. Or think about some of your favorite food memories—maybe a birthday, a vacation, a restaurant, or a family tradition will inspire your next flavor idea. Write them below. Don't hold back! What tastes good to someone else might not taste good to you. And that's ok! Really focus on what you love.

How could you turn one of these ideas into an ice cream treat? What inclusions, which are things like cookie crumbles or sauces, could help you recreate this flavor? Brainstorm some combinations below.

Example: I love having a cup of hot chocolate after ice skating outside during winter break.

Chocolate ice cream + chocolate chips + cinnamon + marshmallow fluff

Check the list of popular inclusions on pg 19 for more ideas!

When we test this recipe, we'll first create a vanilla or a chocolate ice cream base. Which base best fits your idea? Circle one.

vanilla   chocolate

Circle what color (or colors!) your ice cream will be. We can always add food coloring!

brown	black	yellow	blue
green	white	red	teal
orange	purple	pink	gray

Now start brainstorming a name for your flavor. Your name could include a color, food, flavor, place, or anything else you can dream up.

Example: Scoop-de-Loop

Draw what your scoop will look like so customers know what to expect when they buy it at the store.

How tall will your scoop be?

Will you add extras like whipped cream or a cherry on top?

Is the cone plain or would you add nuts or sprinkles?

Create a design
for your flavor on
this pint container.
Make sure to
include the name of
your flavor.

Write your final ingredient combination and flavor name
below.

My ice cream flavor is called _____.

It's a chocolate / vanilla base.

It has _____ flavoring.

Inside, you'll find pieces of _____, bits of
_____, and some _____.

It was inspired by _____.

Now it's time to test out your flavor idea! First, we'll mix up an ice cream base that can be made without an ice cream machine. We'll add vanilla or chocolate flavoring then finish with your inclusions. Let's get started!

HERE'S EVERYTHING YOU WILL NEED:

- 1 14 ounce can of sweetened condensed milk
- ¼ cup evaporated milk
- 2 Large mixing bowls
- 2 cups cold heavy whipping cream
- Hand mixer
- Spatula
- Freezer-safe storage container with lid

For a VANILLA base:
2 tsp vanilla extract

For a CHOCOLATE base:
3 tbsp cocoa powder

For your flavor:

Whatever inclusions, flavoring, and food coloring that you need! For liquid inclusions, like jelly or sauce, add ¼ cup. For solid inclusions, like crumbles, add ½ cup. For flavoring, add ½ to 1 tsp. For food coloring, add 1-2 drops.

CREATE YOUR BASE

1. Add sweetened condensed milk and evaporated milk to a large mixing bowl and stir.

2. Now stir in either vanilla extract or cocoa powder (depending on if you want your ice cream base to be flavored with chocolate or vanilla).

3. If you'd like to add additional flavoring, for example mint flavoring, add ½-1 teaspoon now and stir well.

4. If you'd like to add food coloring, add 1-2 drops now. Stir well.

5. Now it's time for inclusions! Add ¼ cup of inclusions like jelly or sauce and ½ cup of inclusions like cookie crumbles.

6. Using a hand mixer, whip the cold heavy whipping cream in a large bowl on medium high until the liquid turns into whipped cream. It should take about three minutes.

7. Using a spatula, gradually add the whipped cream to the milk mixture. Gently fold the whipped cream into the milk mixture until they are combined.

TIME TO FREEZE

1. Using the spatula, pour the ice cream base into the storage container. Add the lid.

2. Let freeze for at least six to eight hours.

3. Remove from the freezer, and scoop into a bowl.

4. If it's too firm, let it sit on the counter fo ra few minutes. Then try scooping again.

Tasting time! What did you think of your creation? What would you change next time? Let friends and family give it a try and gather their opinions. What flavor should you create next? Write your notes below.

MORE RECIPES FOR ICE CREAM

Cookies and Cream: add ½ cup crushed up chocolate sandwich cookies to a vanilla base

Unicorn: add 1 drop of red, blue, and yellow food coloring plus ¼ cup of rainbow sprinkles to a vanilla base

PB&J: add 1 cup slightly warm peanut butter and ¼ cup strawberry jelly to a vanilla base

Brownie Burst: add 2 tbsp sugar plus ½ cup crumbled brownies to a chocolate base

S'Mores: add ½ cup crushed up graham crackers, ¼ cup mini chocolate chips, and a sprinkle of mini marshmallows on top of a vanilla base

Mint Chocolate Chip: add ½ tsp peppermint extract, 1 drop green food coloring, and ¼ cup mini chocolate chips to a vanilla base

Strawberry Pie: add ½ cup crushed up graham crackers, ¼ cup chopped up strawberries, and 1 drop of pink food coloring to a vanilla base

HERE'S A TIP!

To easily crush up cookies or nuts, place them in a zip-top bag then tap them gently with a spoon until they crumble.

CHAPTER 6
LOOK UP!

WHY WE LOOK UP TO DR. MAYA

SHE'S HAPPY.

Dr. Maya's energy is contagious! She chose a job that brings joy and inspiration to her life every day.

SHE'S UNIQUE.

Dr. Maya became an ice cream scientist even though she had never met one before. She wasn't afraid to be the first.

SHE'S PASSIONATE.

Ice cream is Dr. Maya's lifestyle. Just look at her ice cream shoes, ice cream blazer, ice cream pajamas...

SHE'S GIVING.

Dr. Maya is always looking for ways to share her talents with others and to give back to her community.

SHE'S ADVENTUROUS.

Dr. Maya has traveled all over the world for work and for fun. She never leaves home without her smile or her curiosity.

What are some things that you are passionate about?

Talk about a cause that is important to you.

List three things that inspire you.

Describe a time you went exploring in a new place.

Talk about a time when you helped others who were younger than you.

When have you done something that no one else did before?

ℓ LOOK UP MORE! ℓ

There's so much more to learn. If any of the topics in this book inspired you, head to the library to find more information or ask an adult to help you search online. Here are some ideas to get you started.

CHEMISTRY

The American Chemical Society's Adventures in Chemistry website shares lots of fun experiments, games, and more! (**acs.org/content/acs/en/education/whatischemistry/ adventures-in-chemistry.html**)

FOOD SCIENCE

The Exploratorium, a science museum in San Francisco, shares tons of fun food science experiments online. Watch the videos at **exploratorium.edu/video/collections/ hungry-for-science**.

TRAVEL

One of Dr. Maya's biggest passions—besides ice cream—is travel. Learn how you can start thinking like an explorer by reading American Girl's A Smart Girl's Guide to Travel by Aubre Andrus. Lonely Planet Kids also creates great books about our amazing world.

ABOUT THE EXPERT

Dr. Maya is an Ice Cream Scientist with a PhD from the University of Wisconsin-Madison in Food Science, specializing in the microstructure, sensorial, and behavioral properties of frozen aerated desserts. She is also part of the winning duo (#SweetScientists) from the 25th season of the Emmy Award-winning reality show, The Amazing Race (alongside her friend and former lab mate, Dr. Amy DeJong). Currently, Dr. Maya oversees Research and Product Development for SMiZE Cream as the official SMiZE Cream Ice Cream Scientist. Follow her at **drmayawarren.com** and **@maya.warren**.

ABOUT THE AUTHOR

Aubre Andrus is an award-winning children's book author with dozens of books published by American Girl, National Geographic Kids, Lonely Planet Kids, Disney, Scholastic, and more. Her titles encourage kids to be kind and be curious, and she is committed to writing books that empower girls and inspire them to become the leaders of tomorrow. Aubre received her degree in journalism and film from the University of Wisconsin. She currently lives in Los Angeles with her husband and daughter. Visit her website at **aubreandrus.com**.

WHO'S NEXT?

Meet Angella, a beauty chemist who literally mixes science with nature to create lotions, potions, and polishes that bring people joy everyday.

Meet Zi, a video game developer who was an artist before she was an engineer. Zi uses technology to transform ideas into games that entertain people around the world.

Parents and educators, visit **thelookupseries.com** to see who you can meet next and to find video interviews, free downloads, and more.

Made in the USA
Columbia, SC
18 December 2021

52037808R00035